SERIAL BOOKS
Architecture & Urbanism 5

ARMED SURFACES

Dagmar Richter
DR_D

Introduction by Andrew Benjamin
Edited by Miriam Kelly

Black Dog Publishing

DR_D

The DR_D Organisation is an experimental design enterprise which is closely linking research with applied concrete operations in our contemporary culture through a continuous effort to redefine spatial performance criteria in response to changing cultural conditions, political critique and theoretical discourse. Consequently, the DR_D group has undertaken to combine architectural theory, spatial and cultural analysis, dynamic modelling programmes, temporal events and infra-structural requirements to develop and constantly test a diagram for performing surfaces, to replace standardised functions or pre-designed architectural compositions. These investigations have produced a number of prototypes directly related to the re-definition of performance standards.

The Design Research Development Laboratory — DR_D Lab — is connected to a research studio at the Art Academy Stuttgart and investigates design processes, their ideologies and formal rules, independent of programmatic and commercial constraints. In Santa Monica, California, the DR_D Studio uses international competitions and invited exhibitions to apply the Lab's research. The DR_D Office in Berlin operates as a testing ground for commercially viable production from the renovation and construction of small buildings to the creation of furniture and objects which are rapidly prototyped.

CONTENTS

Performing, Effecting Surfaces · Andrew Benjamin · 6

Armed Surfaces — Towards a New Topology · Dagmar Richter · 10

DomestiCITY · 16

The Wave · 28

Waterford · 38

The Dom-in(f)o House · 48

PERFORMING, EFFECTING SURFACES
Andrew Benjamin

"Art in its highest exaltation hates exegesis; it therefore immediately shuns the emphasis on meaning."

Gottfried Semper

As lines knot intensities emerge that begin to take on the possibility of form. These lines are as much the marks of movement as they are the conveyors of information. To be precise, of course, the lines neither mark nor convey – they are movement and information. Understanding this shift – a shift in which a structure of representation is displaced by another conception of the line – forms an integral part of what is necessary to the work of Dagmar Richter. Once lines are given the extension they need such that they come to define a field of activity, then rather than a line which can do no more than mark the distance between two points, they acquire the quality of a surface.

The work presented here forms a fundamental part of a specific trajectory within contemporary architectural practice. As opposed to the production of computer generated surfaces that are then given volumetric expression, there is the use of what will be described as the surface effect – Richter's 'performing surfaces'. As is made clear in the texts accompanying the project descriptions, the lineage of this approach runs from at least Semper, through Loos, up to the present. But, while having certain accuracy, such a formulation would misconstrue the history involved and thus fail to grasp the significance of this work. Rather than the passage of time leading to the current situation, something else is at stake. With the development of computer software that allows for the construction of surfaces that work to distribute elements of architecture as much as programme and programmable space, there is a different exigency. What these developments demand is a recasting of the history such that a history of the surface can be written from the position of the present.

Semper's insistence on a distinction between the wall as that which brings about spatial enclosure and the wall as load bearing redefines the wall's presence. Once the wall's presence is no longer reducible to the literal wall, it attains a freedom such that it is possible to talk of 'the wall effect'. And once this position is connected to his writings on textiles and materials, what emerges is an undertaking that links the project of architecture and its realisation to the work of materials. What is important, however is that those materials have the capacity to define the particularity of a given project by positioning the surface as distributing programme. To the extent that the wall effect can be realised by the work of the surface it is also possible that the surface can distribute other foundational architectural elements. There is no a priori reason, for example, to think that furniture cannot be an effect of the surface. Once the surface becomes productive, and this is the potential that is there in Semper, though equally in Loos for whom the intersection of the 'Raumplan' and cladding opens up the work of the surface effect, another history of architecture becomes possible.

Architects, of whom Richter is one, who begin with the surface — the surface as productive and thus defined in terms of becoming — can move between an interest in the surface, the computer generated surface as a diagram, and the way materials can combine to create literal surfaces that effect. The surface involves therefore two dimensions, the surface as diagram and the surface as material enactment. They combine in particular ways in given projects.

The presence of the surface as a diagram allows for specific modes of investigation. In DomestiCITY the rigid distinction between public and private, where the presence of walls defines the limits of the possible, is overcome by acts of architectural extension. By distributing functions and thus reprogramming spaces as at once private and public, the dispersed subject has a home. While the house retains its particularity, the spread of personal activities through apparently 'public' space and the inscription of the activities of the complex subjectivity of modernity into the house is enacted through the drawing of lines of dispersal through and across urban fields. At this level there is generality and yet it is precisely because there is an abstract form of the general that there can be particularisation. If this is prototyping then it has taken a unique form. Rather than the model of the trainer or the automobile, here there is actual singularity. Prototyping has to break with a conception of production that is delimited by the reiteration, no matter how intricate, of Sameness. The real strength of this project lies, in part, in Richter's insistence on the copresence of the 'unique' — it is after all my house — and the recognition that permanence has become impermanence. The latter need not be literal. There is no need for what she calls the 'nomadic generation' to be without any sense of place. Rather the relationship between the domestic and the urban — beautifully captured in the term DomestiCITY — is redefined by performing surfaces that weave together what were initially understood as mutually exclusive terms. These weaves create diagrams. The move to form — the diagram's architectural resolution — is not to construe the diagram volumetrically. Performing surfaces are as much an analysis as suggestive of a resolution that will necessitate realising abstraction's inherent potential.

The Waterford Crystal project once again deploys the interplay of surface and diagram. In this instance instead of starting with a surface that carried information in any straightforward sense, the material surface of crystals became the point of departure. There are two elements of this approach that need to be noted, both attest to the power of Richter's work. The first concerns what will be described as the necessity for interruption and the second, architectural experimentation. Experimentation, as will be suggested, deploys the relationship between the abstract and the particular. However, it should be noted that it is not the relationship between the universal and the particular, since such a mode of thinking is antithetical to the work of diagrams and surfaces that characterise Richter's recent projects.

One of the problems inherent in constructing surfaces through the use of animation software is defining the point at which the animation should be brought to an end. The risk of formalism lies in the absence of a constraint that is external to the logic of the animation itself. While one way of interrupting such a procedure can occur by the use of a programmatic diagram that intersects the volumetric one, Richter intersects the immateriality of the computer generated surface via an engagement with physical surfaces and their inherent constraints. Hair and crystals provided sites of investigation in order to identify properties that would allow for points of intersection between the material and the immaterial to be noted. While the use of crystals bears an important connection to the history of Waterford, the property of the crystals themselves was just as indispensable in allowing for the creation of productive surfaces.

Once constraints can be established, then instead of this resulting in finished products, it needs to be understood as creating sites in which both models and ideas can be tested. The re-presentation of Waterford as a complex object of mirrored surfaces results from the interplay of the immaterial and the material. Instead of there having been the rush to finality — as though either a simple analysis or an elementary animation are generative of built form — Waterford re-emerged as a diagram that was able to incorporate architectural interventions. The surface did not function as an image guiding the project. Richter deployed different senses of the surface to recreate, for architecture, Waterford as a diagram. This level of abstraction was the condition allowing for a specific intervention. Once again, the prototype attains particularity and thus can address the concerns of a given town or region only on the precondition of abstraction.

A similar strategy can also be found in the Dom-in(f)o House. Prior to noting — albeit briefly — the particularity of that research project, it is essential to reiterate the significance of this undertaking. As has already been intimated, contemporary research in architecture can be driven by form creation to the point where it circles back upon itself to meet work occurring under the rubric of 'form follows function'. In both instances the dominance of form creation make programmatic concerns devoid of specificity. At no point could these concerns be allowed to have any impact on form creation.

Richter's move is from Le Corbusier's Domino House, which she views as restricting architectural intervention to no more than the cladding or aestheticising of an 'engineered architecture', to the Dom-in(f)o House in which the surface is present as structure.

While this is a move that is occasioned by initially rendering the skeleton through the application of animation software, the smooth relations that are then constructed cannot be viewed as ends in themselves. Indeed, the contrary is the case. The transformation means that the House is now a site in which different modalities of habitation — polis dwelling — can be tested. While the tests are formal in nature, each formal transformation is intended to open up for evaluation other possibilities for housing and living. Here, Richter emerges as an architect of the political, rather than as a merely political architect.

Part of what is demonstrated here is the limitation of the apparent freedom of the Domino frame. Only the transformations resulting from the smoothing of the elements allows it to be 'bombarded with contemporary performance criteria'. As such, new domestic and social conditions can be investigated from within the activity of design itself.

Dagmar Richter's work opens up a way beyond the formalism in which the appearance of the architecture of animation software is simply the realisation of the diagram and thus is the effacing of the diagrammatic. Equally, it allows for programme to be central to production. It is not surprising that she always connects — perhaps inter-articulates — experimentations with surfaces and political, cultural and theoretical concerns. Surfaces perform, when they allow. Surfaces effect, when they realise. Allowing and realising are modes of freedom that have to be marked by actuality. They are not the idealised freedoms that the oscillation between utopianism and formalism enacts. Rather, they involve the creation of openings that create different possibilities by giving them a place. How they are then lived with, is the question that makes the future, even if unpredictable, a concern of the present.

ARMED SURFACES Towards a New Topology
Dagmar Richter

"But the artist, the architect, first senses the effect that he intends to realize and sees the rooms he wants to create in his mind's eye. He senses the effect that he wishes to exert upon the spectator.... These effects are produced by both the material and the form of the space."[1]

Adolf Loos

Le Corbusier asserted that a revolution in the production of space, represented by the icon of his Dom-ino House, had already taken place at the start of the twentieth century. Mass production was widely embraced in Western Europe and America, but despite efforts in the 1960s and behind the Iron Curtain during the post War period, the discipline of architecture largely resisted the global impetus and remained ideologically committed to the notion of permanence and customisation. By insisting that each built object remain a laborious construct for one timeless singularity, a critical aspect of spatial production was excluded from the architectural lexicon. In distinguishing building from architecture, architecture became increasingly distanced from everyday life. Contemporary experiments in standardised housing have therefore failed to realise the promise of a higher standard of living, often leaving underprivileged inhabitants to exist in a sub-urban and spatial no-man's-land and not in a space which, as Le Corbusier had hoped, would touch and elate them.

The structural reading of post War architectural material, represented in the traditional plan or section, relied on the common understanding that the 'thing as such' was the weight and presence of the building mass. In order for architects to appear ethical and truthful, sectional material presence was ideologically required in their system of representation. In urban design the same ideological construct prevailed as the city was defined and ordered through a reading of figure/ground.

When Adolf Loos questioned the material presence of architectural space in 1898, he echoed Semper, writing some 40 years before. In tracing the origins of classical architecture to techniques of knotting, fabricating and plant weaving, Semper and Loos postulated that a woven or knotted surface, providing shade and delineating space and ownership, already exercised a fundamental architectural effect and therefore constituted the basis from which the mythical conception of architecture could have emerged.

Contemporary technological development once more relieves the wall of its traditional function as a constructive element providing only security and climatic control. Today, surfaces are modelled using computer technology to delineate space and texture-mapping to veneer a chosen fabric directly onto the modelled architectural surfaces. We can again take delight with Semper and Loos in the word play of 'Wand' (wall) and 'Gewand' (dress) to argue for a linguistic proof of origin, identifying in English the word 'textile' in texture mapping.[2]

"This transformation of what could be called poché from an inert mass between forms, or as something from which void is cut, and to something highly mobile and volatile can be seen as the subversion of the form of both traditional solids and their traditional organisation in space."[3]

As Peter Eisenman stated so clearly a century after Loos, the question of form — its origin, inception and the techniques ultimately used to derive materiality in architecture — always demands repeated examination and can again unravel, with the help of linguistic and structural investigations, a conceptual beginning. The Semperian argument, furthered by so many since, repeatedly challenged the status quo and perpetually advanced an architecture capable of operating on/as the surface.

The concept of architecture as surface is advanced and reaffirmed in contemporary digital design and production techniques. It has moved beyond the decorative, postmodern building surface as an applied veneer on a pochéed structure. I would argue that surface, in its current interpretation is, in addition to its many other qualities, also structural and has become the core of the matter.

The computer facilitates the production of increasingly sophisticated spatial renderings, animations and dynamic three-dimensional models, shifting the point of departure for architectural design to the surface and leaving behind the 'depth' implied in an understanding of construction and material. Surface has supplanted construction as the structuring principle of architecture, and the resultant space has evolved as ground against ground in its topological definitions, or figure against figure in its urbanistic renderings.

"Modernity was an organised distrust of the senses. Today we are told by depthless surfaces to trust our senses again. The modernist insight went into depth, was revelatory, and tore off the veil from appearances — today we search for the meaning of surface on the surface. That is why we are changing our style of perception: instead of reaching into the depths, we are surfing on the crests of the waves."[4]

Norbert Bolz

The new generation of architectural authors has grown up in physically static and standardised spaces of apartment complexes, tract houses and high-rises, surrounded by a vast field of media surfaces which shift their view toward the virtual and describe an essentially fluid world of surface. Armour-like, this surface now wields the image — occupying the foreground, delineating our spatial understanding and ordering our immediate world.

Rather than Fröbelian games involving building blocks directly linked to the manipulation, addition and sequential ordering of basic geometric forms, the postmodern child is glued to a screen. The screen bombards the viewer with images of permanent fluidity as characters, their impersonators and virtual playmates are released from physical limitations to swim through fluid space and time, die and be effortlessly re-born. The surfaces surrounding them are electronic, non-material, protective shields — the surface has become the armour.

Through the replay of media-constructed space, a conceptual change is realised from the modernist notion of mass-produced and standardised space of permanence to a space of speed in which shape and reference shift constantly. This is the stuff dreams are made of and the site where desires are sublimated, ordered and experienced. As the computer initiates a new era of spatial production, architecture again reverts to its original identity as surface — to the 'effect' of Loos and Semper.

The new architectural authors started to experiment with unfamiliar software directly linked to the production and animation of surfaces for film and computer games. Random but mathematical statistical material was initially used as the basis for surface animation programmes and a design process was evolved. The passive acceptance of statistical information gradually resulted in an architecture of smoothness which largely lacked cultural or dynamic resistance or friction. Flows of traffic, people and objects were rendered easily manageable and became the raw material of animation. An ideology that shifts authority from culturally responsive discourse to an apparently neutralised function of pure infra-structural performance is problematic since the visual and aesthetic effect of the animated surface has been used as the base for architectural expression.

"... the purpose of construction is to hold together, of architecture to move us."[5]

This assertion has perhaps been taken too literally and unhindered movement and smooth passage have become the often unconscious stated goals of architecture. When Schinkel contemplated the effect of pure functionalism in 1862, he already recognised that the ignorance of the historic and poetic results in the loss of 'freedom' and therefore the political and cultural.[6] As 'blob architecture' emerged as a new style, it did not decrease friction to movement, but denied its cultural responsibility through styling movement patterns through the inherent formal vocabulary of computer programmes.

Surface animations are based on an aesthetic closely tied to the author's multiple, fluid, filmic, media experiences which also carry the burden of their historical understanding and poetic fantasy. Now the simulation of dynamic logic has suddenly become a 'painterly' project, returning to the brink of the nineteenth century, where the painterly approach of the Baroque was considered by Heinrich Wölfflin to constitute the injury of architecture.[7] Ultimately it is exactly the painterly aspect that has become the material architecture is made of, and the figure that can carry, as Le Corbusier demanded, the burden of poetry, history and emotional experience.

The body, its desires and requirements, returns to haunt us as the biological machine that only partly constitutes 'reality', that constructs the real as simulated. Here, mechanisation takes no command, and the performance criteria for the biological machine, for a machine to live in has developed into a sophisticated field of pulsating conditions dynamically affecting multiple realities.

"... the body endured as an ineliminable remainder and therefore constant reminder in so far as the body – operating as it does in terms of feeling, pleasure, resemblance, etc. – remains as the continual source of error and deception...."[8]

Andrew Benjamin

Even the Self beyond its biological body has experienced a substantial overhaul.

"The Self (Subject) is not the 'inner kernel' of an organism, but a surface effect: that is, a 'true' human Self in a sense functions like a computer screen. What is 'behind' it is nothing but a network of 'selfless' neuronal machinery."[9]

Slavoj Žižek

Today, Le Corbusier's *Three Elements of Architecture* – mass, surface and plan – have been entirely redefined and their interrelationships reversed. Mass can no longer be described as the element by which our senses perceive and measure and are most fully affected. Surface, originally merely the envelope of the mass which can diminish or enlarge the sensation the latter gives us, is now perceived and measured most fully by our senses while mass is only capable of enlarging or diminishing this originating force. The plan, once an image of permanence, clarity and strength, has been reformulated into the diagram that is adaptable to temporary conditions in response to the dynamism of contemporary life.

If we first accept the notion that the animation and modelling of surfaces is in all actuality a contemporary pure and total concept of architectural construction, then the morphed and folded surface creates architectural space and its visual delineation in a critical sense. The architectural space of this new century has been entirely redefined through the computer design process, this now standard tool of representation. The architecture of the line, section and heavy material presence and its legible representation — of construction and strength through material presence — has been transformed into an architecture of surface, lightness, mutability, transparency, translucency and transgression. The cultural reference of the new authors has also changed substantially. Media — pictorial and animated as well as filmic surface representation — create an overwhelmingly dominant cultural resource that directly influences animation and spatial construction.

For the DR_D members, the concept of 'armed surface' has therefore become the primary structure in architectural design. The concept of surface as structure and primary experiential mass — the armoured surface — includes multiple performance criteria from the constructive, technical and atmospheric to the cultural, political, poetic, visual and tactile. The original concept of a 'practical aesthetic' invoked by Semper has lost none of its relevance.

1. Loos, Adolf, *Spoken into the Void: Collected Essays 1897-1900*, trans., Jane O.Newman and John H. Smith, Cambridge, MA: MIT Press, 1982, p. 66.

2. The German word *Wand* (wall) acknowledges its origins. The terms *Wand* and *Gewand* (dress) derive from a single root and indicate the woven material that formed the wall.

3. Eisenman, Peter, 1988.

4. Bolz, Norbert, *Design des Immateriellen in Sehnsucht; Über die Veränderung der visuellen Washrnehmug*, Schriftreihe Forum vol. 4, Göttingen: Steidl Verlag, 1955. This translation by Janet Ward appears in her book *Weimar Surfaces: Urban Visual Culture in 1920s Germany*, London: University of California Press, 2002, p. 5 — a text which helped me to clarify my interest in surface.

5. Le Corbuiser, *Vers Une Architecture*, trans., Frederick, Etchells, Oxford Architectural Press, 1987, p. 23.

6. Karl Friedrich Schinkel warned that if functionalism is given first priority, it results in the conceptual lack of poetry and history and therefore freedom. Schinkel, Friedrich, *Nachlass*, herausgegeben bon Freiherr von Wolzogen, Berlin: 1862/1863, Bd. 11, p. 211.

7. Wölfflin, Heinrich, *Das Wesen der Stilwandlung; Renaissance und Barok*, 1888, p. 16.

8. Benjamin, Andrew, *Architectural Philosophy*, London: Athlone Press, 2000, p. 177.

9. Žižek, Slavoj, *Zizek Reader: Of Cells and Selfs*, eds., E. Wright and E. Wright, Oxford Blackwell Publishers, 1999, p 312.

DomestiCITY

Project Credit	DR_D Studio, Santa Monica
Design Principal	Dagmar Richter
Assistants	Markus Sohst, Anthony Guida, Nina Yoon, and Andrew Obermeyer
Date	Summer 2000
Project Description	Research project for UCLA and Armand Hammer Museum

BIG BROTHER

Inside the 'reality TV' house the lives of the incarcerated contestants are constantly documented in intimate detail by an armoury of concealed cameras. As the interior and its occupants are openly scrutinised, the house approaches a condition of full disclosure, confounding its supposed nature as private and distinct from the public realm. The un-private house comes to exist only in relation to its mental field and a complex re-configuration of the concept of house begins to emerge.

THE UN-PRIVATE HOUSE AND THE UN-PUBLIC REALM

Just as the public world invades the house, so — in the domestic settings and nomenclature of restaurants, bar lounges, morning TV talk shows, Internet home pages and advertising companies — the home comes to the world outside. The loss of a public realm to private, corporate space, mourned during the latter half of the twentieth century by traditional urbanists, has in turn yielded to an open, urban field of private and public, of domestic experiences intimately enmeshed with public display and networked by the automobile, airplane, telephone and Internet.

Some of us are still struck by moments in which we find others transgressing the 'rules' of public space — appearing at the library or supermarket in bedroom slippers and curlers. For the locally dynamic and globally connected, groceries ordered online are delivered to the garden for the barbecue, personal possessions are distributed throughout the world in self-storage units, retired relatives live part-time in a Las Vegas hotel and the best home cooking can be had at Joe's. The world now is our home.

Our contemporary culture has thoroughly domesticised the city, where the functions, comforts and conveniences, sensations and even memories of home are available outwith the house. No longer can the house be considered the irreducible unit or fundamental building block of the city's composition. Its boundaries have not merely been permeated or blurred, they have expanded to include the entire world.

airport lounge

location

LOCATION, LOCATION, LOCATION

With domesticity now 'outside the box', each household, by virtue of its position in the artificial classification system which defines postal address, zip code and telephone number, comes to inscribe a domestic situation in the urban field. The purest distillation of a particular point of reference has become the non-reproducible physical site as a unique point in the field. Each one of these points contains an individual frame of reference for the constructed collection of artefacts accumulated by an inhabitant. As an interface between the real and the virtual, this unique physical location is required for the official credit card address, the delivery of amazon.com parcels and the subscription to mobile phone and on-line services.

3-D model of practiced house

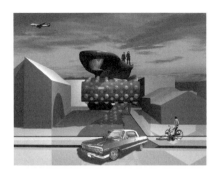

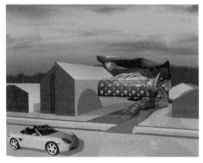

Privacy may no longer be attached to individualism, but site or location is attached to uniqueness. The private house is the centre that receives and transmits, translates and is interpreted by the world. It remains the origin of an identity, of a unique subjectivity in the world.

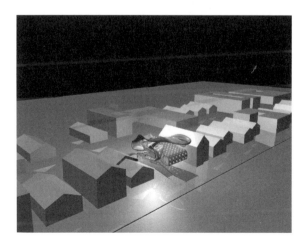

front yard

THE FREE HOUSE

What remains of the private house is the site — a unique address and location from which to welcome good friends and one's part-time children who come to visit. Domesticity is delineated through the front and back yards, where the residual pet comes to denote a perception of home.

The front yard wraps through the house but remains the site of representation, displaying an occupant's sense of order, wealth and personality through the constructed picture window. The front yard is released and allowed to expand into an entire three-dimensional façade for the containment and exhibition of the collection of authentic goods, inherited or purchased, which are assimilated in order to construct an occupant's biography. Here, architecture serves as background supporting the unique and carefully assembled biography, offering it to the potentially interested via the web-cam or to visitors keen to physically engage with the inhabitant.

back yard

The backyard is free to support the few daily rituals still conducted on site such as gardening, barbecues or hanging out with the few remaining personal friends and still-remembered children. The rest of the house has moved into the city and defines itself anew every day as chosen rituals change. One has breakfast at Starbucks, dinner at Joe's, meets the personal trainer at the beach and one's lover in the hotel room. The house plan has therefore become flexible, unrestricted and truly free. Unencumbered by daily functional performance and historical obligation as shelter, the resulting architecture remains a vehicle for representation, in order to arouse aesthetic delight and present the lifestyle of the year.

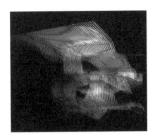 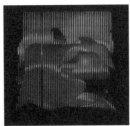 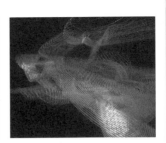

This house of the new nomadic generation is constructed through performing surfaces constantly recycled and redefined in response to the particular desires of the temporary inhabitant. Home or house is adaptable and rapidly prototyped, a performing landscape in a suburban field, constantly evolving in response to change and primarily a surface of representation and delight.

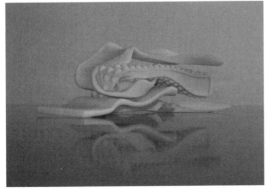

3-D print model

The Wave

Project Credit	DR_D Studio, Santa Monica
Design Principal	Dagmar Richter
Project Manager and Assistant	Markus Sohst, Sean Lally, Nina Yoon
Date	Spring and Summer 2001
Project Description	International competition and conceptual research project

The Wave forms part of the FRAC Centre collection.

The Wave considers strategies of engagement with extra large spaces which, in their structure and identity, have become abstracted from urban and historical reference and reorientated in terms of a topological definition of surface.

In the outskirts of Aalborg, a provincial town in northern Denmark, American style strip-malls intermingle with imitation medieval Viking farmhouses. German tourists rent cheap summerhouses along the coast, but in winter months the harsh climate and inadequate transportation links to major centres outside the town perpetuate its marginalisation.

At the town's periphery the visitor finds a group of very large volumes containing sports facilities of Olympic size, but constructed on a small town budget. Beyond the label 'extra large', these incongruous forms display no discernible reference to the surrounding built environment.

An international competition solicited proposals for an outdoor sports landscape and organisational strategy integrating a new indoor ice skating rink, swimming complex and multi-functional sports and concert hall for Aalborg. The new facilities would enlarge the two existing sports halls into a multiple sports complex and performance centre surrounded by park(ing) to accommodate cars as well as activities in the landscape such as rollerblading, climbing and agricultural exhibitions.

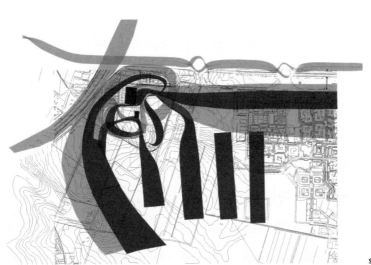

site with vector field

ARMED SURFACES

Through its size and programme, the brief presented a challenge to a typological understanding of architecture and suggested a move towards a topological conceptualisation of surface intended to support predetermined movement patterns and material traits. The new topology had to meet strict performance criteria and was articulated by variations in surface conditions such as temperature fluctuations (changing ice to water to steam), and topographical characteristics (which shifted surfaces from level to undulating to steep). The Wave offered the possibility of developing a complex landscape, both internal and external, whose architectural surfaces supported layered and precise performativities.

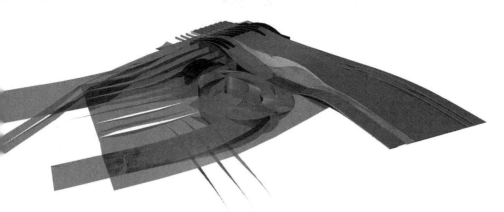

METHOD

The project investigates a methodology that exploits the complex interwoven relationships within the site to influence new performance induced surfaces. The relationships described by a constellation of factors were examined: the topography; surrounding landscape as a cultural construct; its physical environmental, biological and geological processes; and the new proposed sports and entertainment activities as a process of semi-artificial body sculpting. The landscape was no longer regarded as either a natural, given or picturesque image, but rather the entire topography investigated as a dense surface with performative strings attached.

DIAGRAM 1: primary strings

DIAGRAM 2: first layer of interdependent fields

DIAGRAM 3: repeated layering of interdependent fields

The concept unfolded through a process of visualisations, established through animations of dynamic activity zones and climatic energy fields read against static pictorial images and the existing dramatic topography. Using an animation programme, faster and slower movements were channelled through given urban, functional and topographic energy fields. The differential flows reacted through the animation with the topography, existing buildings and present or intended future activities.

The resulting surfaces were repeatedly intensified, thickened and loaded with further performance criteria before being interwoven to create a differentiated, layered topography supporting variations in material, velocity, thermal environment, fluid dynamics and enclosure.

landscape

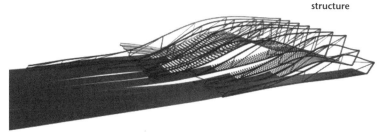

structure

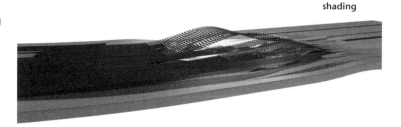

shading

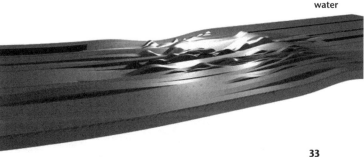

water

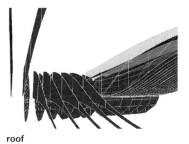

roof

-1

-0

+1

floor plans

FORM

The coloured fluid diagrams established a three-dimensional carpet of interwoven surfaces, emerging in the surrounding landscape and flowing through the existing buildings. The visualisation was then confronted with new statistical data relating to programme, infrastructure and the existing topography. In the resulting dynamic transformations, the fields split and shifted into different layers of possible material presence to evolve a structure of multiple layers and solid/fluid conditions. Gradually a folded, wave-like complex with systematically divergent surfaces emerged, to which distinct performances were assigned. The layered structure was woven back into the surrounding landscape where it supported water management sites, activity fields, parking structures and landscape features.

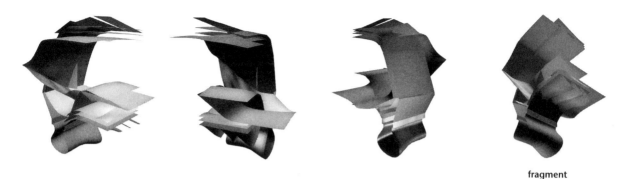

fragment

DESIGN PRODUCTION

Computer-generated information was fed directly into a CNC milling machine to create a three-dimensional working model of the landscape and sectional renderings of the swimming hall. This provided a mechanism of feedback that encouraged constant reconsideration of the proposal and facilitated further control over the experimentation process.

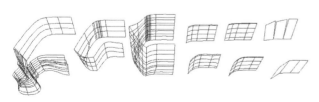

parts

URBAN STRUCTURING

A surface of different consistencies, patterns and shapes was defined as a topographical mega-structure integrating the massive volumes of the existing built objects seamlessly into the landscape. Additional surfaces sheltered and supported activities both indoors and outside throughout the year. New topographical challenges for sledding and snow play as well as horizontal fields for outdoor skating and rollerblading were created, while surfaces were folded and arranged in patterned, planted stripes in order to function as parking lots, skating and roller hockey pitches or concert and exhibition areas. The parking surfaces worked as a buffer-zone and were mostly rendered with tree shading to shelter the site from air and acoustic pollution, strengthened grass areas and strategically placed asphalt planes which also functioned as energy collectors.

The existing path system was retained, shaded and overlapped with loops of secondary paths for cycling, skating and strolling. The paths, new canal, surfaces for storm water management and the many dynamic activities from storage to climbing functioned in different layers, with surfaces arranged according to the types of movement they support. The strategic organisation of large spectator groups was formally and visually integrated into the indoor sports arenas, both existing and new, through a larger topography of smooth and undulating surfaces. The object character of the existing halls has been eliminated in favour for a flowing performative topography.

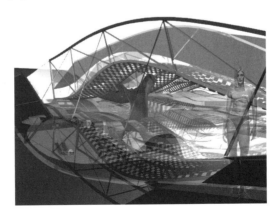

Waterford

Project Credit	Competition entry by DR_D Studio, Santa Monica and further development by DR_D Office, Berlin
Design Principal	Dagmar Richter
Project Manager and Assistant	Dina Krunic
Date	Summer and Autumn 2002
Project Description	International competition and conceptual research project

The predominance of computer animation in the propagation of architectural form over recent years has prompted the DR_D Studio to readdress the concept of physical materiality in the built environment. Deference to the computer during the design process has increasingly impeded engagement with the physical 'facts' of site or programme, which, rather than confirming and enriching the process of digital design, often disrupt a conceptually strong and visually well-defined proposal when introduced at a late stage.

How, then, can the inherent constraints of physical form enter the architectural design process beyond the metaphysical, without compromising the freedom to manipulate space with complex computerised modelling techniques?

Through the Waterford competition, the DR_D Studio has moved away from the electronic manipulation of surface as image and the digital rendering of architecture as fleeting, light and transparent, to investigate physical surfaces as structure and develop an understanding of the project's potential physicality.

waterford site

An international competition for the city of Waterford in Southern Ireland solicited proposals for the reorganisation of an entire city zone. The brief requested a strategy to attract financial investment to the city through the creation of commercial and residential space, a lively new river front with a diverse programme and a signature building which would present a distinctive urban identity to a competitive global market.

Using the substantial background information that accompanied the brief, an urban strategy was advanced that provided a testing ground for new development possibilities in an area facing serious financial challenges. The recent under-investment in the city necessitated the provision of substantial areas of marketable space and the design proposal rapidly emerged as an experimental research project investigating scale, segmentation and variation of form using contemporary production methods for large-scale development.

The competition sought a new development oriented along the northern bank of the River Suir on a site characterised by long pedestrian and cycle paths and a narrow street following the riverbank. An intervention was required to provide a new working infrastructure to connect, facilitate production and entertainment and reflect the identity of the city to the inhabitant, visitor and remote observer.

DESIGN PROCESS

As an alternative point of departure to the computer animation process, the physical nature of collected objects was investigated. An understanding of materiality — including weight and formal resistance — was integrated early in the project's conceptual development to discipline the design process. The erroneous sense of ultimate formal freedom from material matter perpetuated by the computer was gradually undermined through engagement with the physical surfaces and their inherent constraints.

In response to the linear language of the Waterford site, organising elements in the form of smooth, string-like structures, interwoven by secondary tentacles, were proposed. Since their nature and limitations carried some of the physical traits suggested by these organising elements, long hairs were chosen as the physical subjects of the investigation. The hairs were examined as structures both visually and by touch, before being arranged into many configurations and repeatedly scanned. The emerging structures were then tested using computer modelling and animation techniques and applied to the site as organising elements exhibiting specific physical resistances which informed an understanding of the potential material constraints of the architecture.

The resultant model was subsequently confronted by surface studies of glass crystals that carried with them a sense of Waterford's historical identity. The crystal surfaces were studied physically and their reflective properties considered before being collected, scanned, dissected, rearranged and used as a framework to create both form and infra-structural performing surfaces. The design strategy became a process of selection, interpretation, rearrangement and, ultimately, structuring. The physical attributes and inherent resistances of the chosen surfaces were retained and assimilated into the different surface structures during subsequent electronic manipulation.

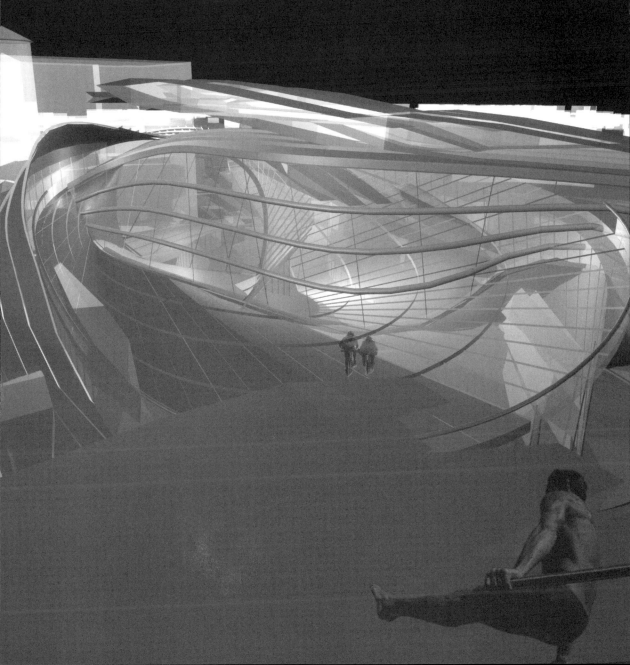

URBAN STRATEGY

The project undertook to create a new surface for the city, presenting Waterford as a complex object of reflecting surfaces, while exploiting the favourable southern orientation of the site and its dramatic views. The proposal began to react to the forces and flow of the river and programme was strategically appropriated through a process in which the linear ordering structures were distorted by water pressure and traffic flows through a series of computer-animated tests.

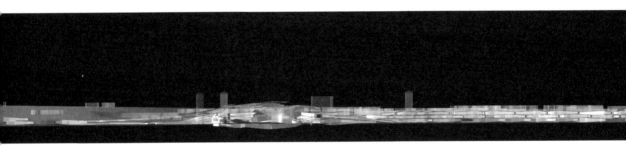

section through new riverfront

The riverfront was organised by linear strings supporting segmented, mass-produced elements accommodating specific programmatic requirements, that converged to form a central, knotted structure. The strands wove along the existing urban infrastructure to provide pedestrian access over the train tracks and across the river. The network would develop new branches to expand over time with the city, unfolding to facilitate specific events and smoothly connecting the different urban layers. A new ferry terminal was proposed to connect the river network with the different programmes along its bank, and cars were organised into the underground parking structure to minimise traffic in the city and liberate space for buildings and public areas. The linear string adjacent to the river accommodated a variety of restaurants, pubs and small public programmes and provided an open breathing space that allowed a certain distance for contemplation as the entire image of the city unfolded to the south.

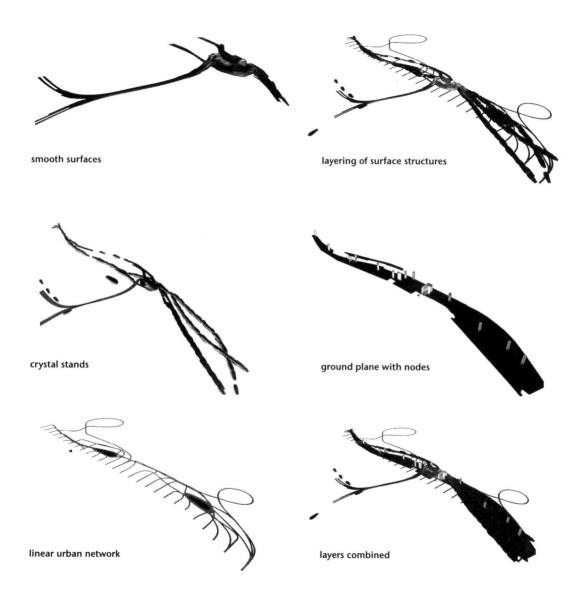

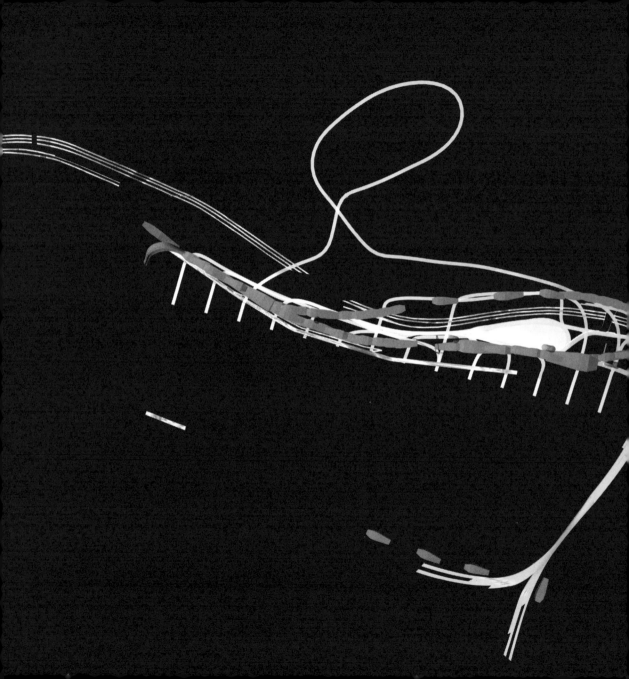

A strategy was developed to support differentiated units accommodating housing, leisure facilities and public amenities. Stacked, mass-produced, crystalline forms were added along the network of linear strands ordering the site. The 250 predetermined, prefabricated 'crystals' of different proportions and variations were designed specifically for production at a modern shipyard. Each unit would be constructed from a prototype cage and a range of interiors applied in response to budget and programme.

A variety of predictable prototype building parts were proposed which combined to create either stackable volumes, or the flattened, folded steel surfaces which were used to construct bridges and the skin of civic buildings. The prototypical elements were to be developed locally in a process of rapid prototyping that enabled the in situ testing of new possibilities in building technology.

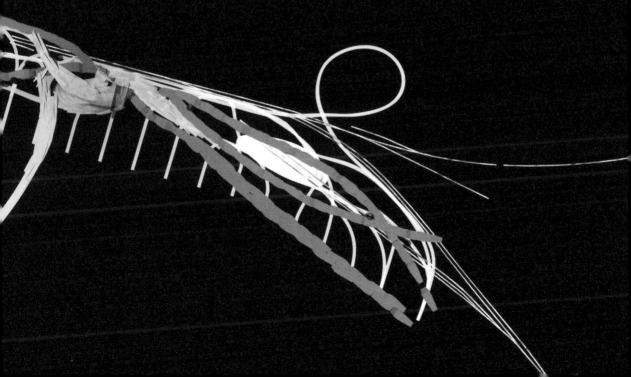

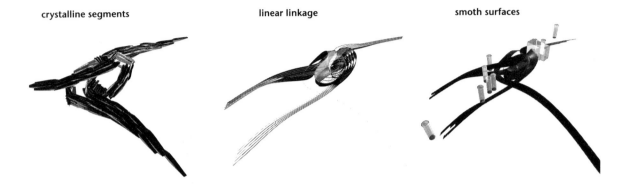

crystalline segments   linear linkage   smoth surfaces

PERFORMANCE BUILDING

A signature building was intended as an urban logo, creating a unique and recognisable global media identity. Through the project, the concept of the building was developed from an object as city signifier to a construction that was simultaneously image, landscape and urban infrastructure.

The building emerged from a knot of structured surfaces, both smooth and crystalline, which through their complex layering and unfolding, provided a public outer surface connecting directly with the pedestrian bridge to the city centre. The building's upper surface functioned as a pedestrian link to the riverbank, while accommodating an open-air theatre and city terrace. Complex surfaces of curved glass articulated a grand foyer below. An indoor theatre was organised by the woven surfaces which delineated flexible seating and stage configurations with a complex lighting and acoustic infrastructure.

performance building interior

The building functioned as a performance centre, accommodating many diverse activities, while providing a focus to the riverbank and expressing through its physical materiality Waterford's historical preoccupation with glass. The surfaces of the building shift into a smooth, transparent topography and crystallise into mass-produced segments creating enclosures for individual programmatic elements.

The urban strategy for Waterford attempts to offer a practical, innovative and economic proposal for a new city front. The project provides a unique foreground composition of reflective surfaces which respond to the river and open up towards the city, behind which a beautiful landscape unfolds.

elevation from Waterford

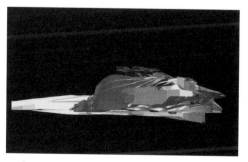

The Dom-in(f)o House

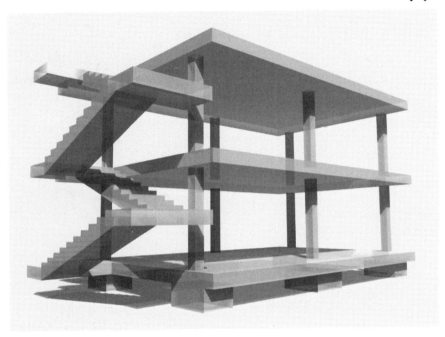

Project Credit	DR_R Lab, Stuttgart Dagmar Richter + Future development DR_R Office, Berlin
Design Principal	Dagmar Richter
Research Director	Jonas Luther
Research Assistants	Martijn Eefting, Erik Hökby, Hartmut Flothmann
Members of the Lab	Dom-in(fo) and Surface Library – Daniela Boog, Ines Klemm, Klaus Kegel, Claudia Kreis, Johannes Pellkofer, Philipp Rehm, Carolin Saile, Michael Scheuerer, Tomoko Oki, Isabell Ziegler
	Surface Library – Florian Frey, Florian Kneer, Boris Koischwitz, Neli Ouzounova, Charlotte Stein
Date	2002-2003
Project Description	Academic Research Project

The co-invention and construction of the 1914 Dom-ino House skeleton evolved in Le Corbusier's own words "a pure and total concept of construction", its inherent success making it an international model of standardisation and mass-production. The prototype, constructed from ferro- or 'armoured' concrete, seemed at first genially simple — forming a general, stackable system of floor plates carried by gritted columns. A free plan was thus facilitated which could support any useful variation and specificity of use. Operating within this framework, the architect could only clad and aestheticise the engineered structure that carried weight and action. Questions of enclosure, ornamentation and site specificity were resigned to the background of the architectural debate in order to facilitate a rapid reconstruction of housing after the First World War.

The Modernist iconic prototype of the Dom-ino skeleton was chosen by the DR_D Lab as a starting point for further spatial exploration and as a mechanism to re-test their hypothesis that the substantial disciplinary definition of architecture today lies in the surface as the pure and total concept of construction.

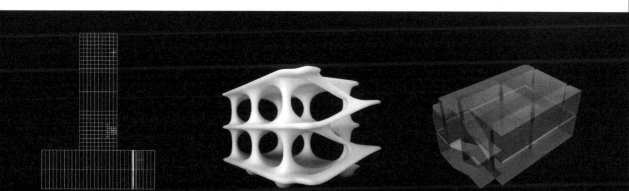

first matrix of computer translations with
performance commands

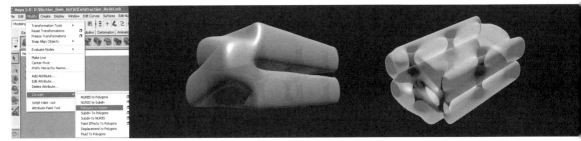

performance command:
convert polygons to sub-division

space model

space model

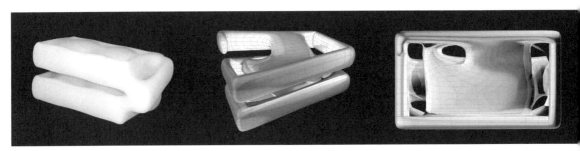

3-D print of space model

performance command: integrate stair

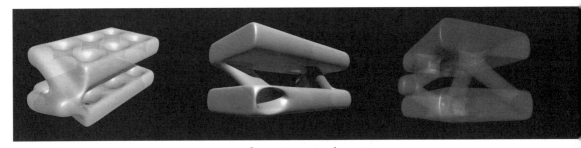

performance command:
connect outside/inside

computer translation of the construction model
towards a sub-division model with internal links

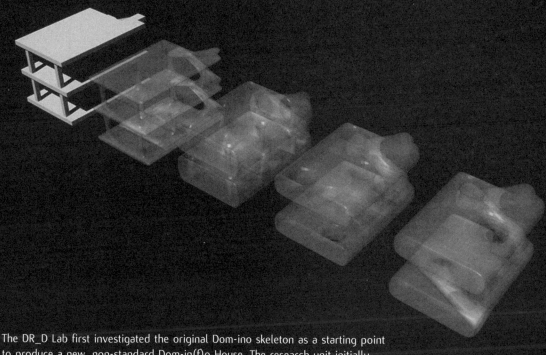

The DR_D Lab first investigated the original Dom-ino skeleton as a starting point to produce a new, non-standard Dom-in(f)o House. The research unit initially produced several investigations analysing the automatic reading of the existing Dom-ino skeleton through surface animation programmes. This process produced many new interpretations resulting in a collection of numerous reconfigured prototypes. The DR_D group made the potentially indefinite and variable nature of the new prototype dependent on the stated performance criteria used as defining parameters, such as connection, non-hierarchical relationships, communication, adaptability and surface as structure.

computer transformations of construction model

Rather than applying conceptual and technical additions to the mass-produced skeleton 'after the fact', performance criteria were used to drive the transformative process of the given surface from the start. The skeleton was permanently challenged with new criteria including atmosphere, humidity, temperature, light and issues of recycling, supply and waste. Where the original Dom-ino House was a direct reaction to standardised skeletal production for inter War housing needs, the contemporary Dom-in(f)o prototype has to produce a spatio-temporal structuring of a society of shrinking cities, permanently shifting densities and new types of living for the different nomadic life cycles of the inhabitants' constructed and permanently reconstructed biography.

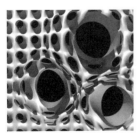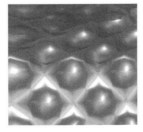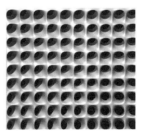

variables from surface library

In the first phase of this research project a new skeleton was evolved. It subsequently underwent a second test phase where different base models were set into largely generalised contextual frameworks. Here, contemporary social data was used to create new housing diagrams for different speeds and velocities. A collection of skeletal prototypes was developed that directly tested and linked the theoretical discussions to a new model for a topology for living.

Two distinct conditions were studied. Firstly, the 'skeleton' of the Dom-in(f)o House was directly linked to the new role given to the architectural surface as a performing surface. Here different diagrams were produced for four basic contextual models, which enabled new combinations of structure and surface, inside and outside, mass-production and adaptability.

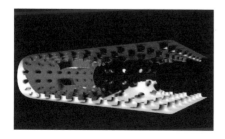 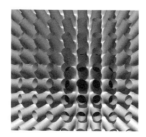 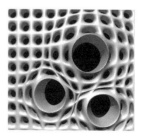

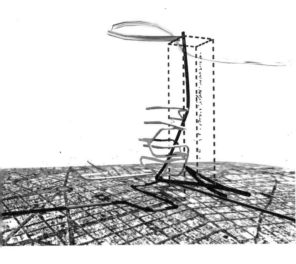

CASE 1: LONG TERM VERTICAL LIVING

diagram of infrastructural interconnections and velocity in Mexico City

PROTOTYPES

distributer

distributer horizontal

fast connector

rester

split rester with fast track

warper

VERTICAL STACKING ABOVE A SUBWAY STATION IN MEXICO CITY

The contextual models studied new ways of living in either dense vertical urban situations or low density horizontal environments. The possibility of high-rise stacking for both long and short term living was tested through abstract scenarios in different metropolitan areas. A dense urban public space was intended to connect all units through vertical urban-scapes. The possibility of low rise housing in single or attached units in generic suburban landscapes was also put forward for short and long term living. New possibilities for connecting the surrounding landscape to the different horizontal units were developed and a leisure oriented environment floating on water was investigated.

In Case 1, long term vertical living above a subway station in Mexico City was studied. Case 2 investigated long term living in the suburb of Weissenhof in Stuttgart, while Case 3 considered short term living for immigrants in the centre of Shanghai. Finally, Case 4 developed a strategy for short term living in the wetlands of Florida.

FRAGMENT 1: elevator

FRAGMENT 2: slow interior

first stacking model for Mexico City

CASE 2: LONG TERM HORIZONTAL LIVING

site plan

Dom-in(f)o skeleton for attachment

inserted prototype

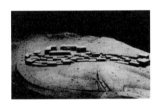

model of Mies van der Rohe's Weissenhof development in Stuttgart

HORIZONTAL ATTACHMENT AT THE SITE OF THE WEISSENHOF DEVELOPMENT IN STUTTGART

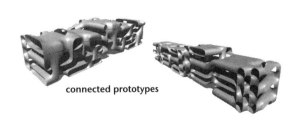

connected prototypes

side elevation

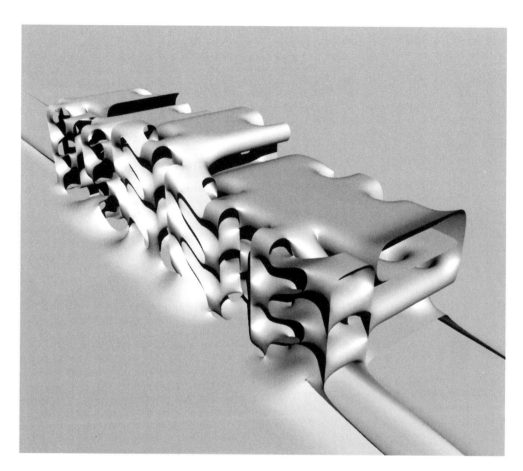

 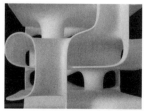 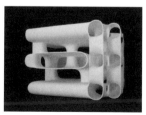 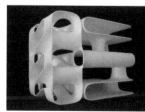

3-D model prints

CASE 3: SHORT TERM VERTIVAL LIVING

unit 1

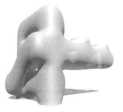
unit 2 - fast

unit 3 - slow

stack units 1 and 2

1 and 2 after vertical stacking

1 and 2 after vertical second stacking

2 base unit

2 units connected

units 1 and 2 connected

VERTICAL STACKING IN THE CENTRE OF SHANGHAI

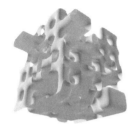

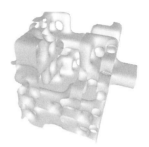

tower in the centre of Shanghai

CASE 4: SHORT TERM HORIZONTAL LIVING

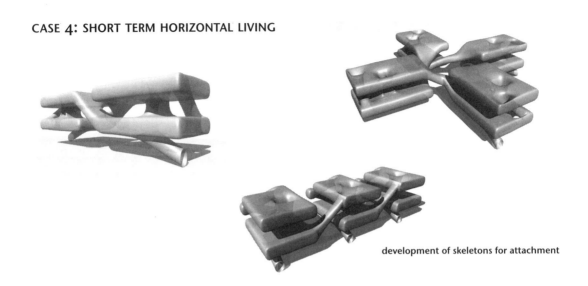

development of skeletons for attachment

HORIZONTAL ATTACHMENTS FOR THE FLORIDA EVERGLADES

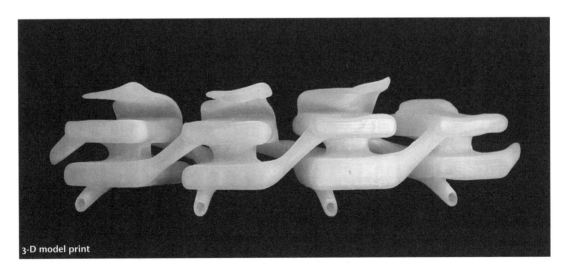

3-D model print

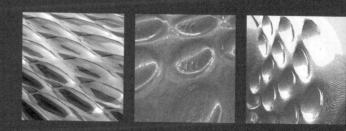

SURFACE LIBRARY

Secondly, the 'veneer' and adaptable 'furnishing' of the Dom-ino House were analysed. The previously chosen fragments from the obtained Dom-in(f)o House were then transformed, enabling a further development through the extensive use of a newly established surface library. This surface library was previously collated through the testing of different performance criteria such as visual access, filtering, shading, body support and ability to contain and use water within a 10 x 10 metre surface. Situations within the different new skeletons were chosen to describe with the help of the selected surfaces different interior perspectives.

The resultant Dom-in(f)o House attempts to describe a new topologic understanding of architecture for contemporary living.

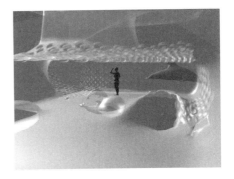

fragmentary situation description

Black Dog Publishing
Architecture Art Design Fashion History Photography Theory and Things

Armed Surfaces © 2004 Black Dog Publishing Limited

All rights reserved. No part of this publication may be reproduced, stored in a retrieval system, or transmitted, in any form or by any means, electronic, mechanical, photocopying. recording or otherwise, without prior permission of the publisher. Every effort has been made to trace the copyright holders, but if any have been inadvertently overlooked the publishers will be pleased to make the necessary arrangements at the first opportunity.

Designed by Emilia Gómez López @ BDP

ISBN 1 901033 39 2

British Library cataloguing-in-publication data
A catalogue record for this book is available from the British Library

Black Dog Publishing Limited
Studio 4.04
Tea Building
56 Shoreditch High Street
London E1 6JJ UK
tel: +44 (0) 20 7613 1922   fax: +44 (0) 20 7613 1944
email: info@bdp.demon.o.uk
www.bdpworld.com

Serial Books: Architecture and Urbanism is supported by Architecture, School of Arts, Culture and Environment, University of Edinburgh.

Architecture School of Arts, Culture and Environment
University of Edinburgh
20 Chambers Street
Edinburgh
EH1 1JZ
fax. +44 (0)131 650 8019

DR_D Lab
Art Academy Stuttgart
Prof. Dagmar Richter
Am Weißenhof 1
D70191 Stuttgart
dagmar.richter@abk-stuttgart.de

DR_D Studio
Dagmar Richter
2640 Highland Ave.
Santa Monica
CA 90405/USA
drichter@ucla.edu

DR_D Office
Dagmar Richter
Rhinower Str. 10
10437 Berlin
dagmar.richter.berlin@freenet.de